RAMAYANA

Part 4

AYODHYA EPISODE-II

PUBLISHED BY

DREAMLAND PUBLICATIONS

J-128, KIRTI NAGAR, NEW DELHI - 110 015
PHONE : 543 5657, 545 5657, FAX : 011-543 8283

Seeing the inhabitants of Ayodhya following him, Ram said to them with folded hands, "I implore you all to return to Ayodhya and extend your fullest co-operation to Bharata, your new king. It will prove your real affection for me."

The people turned a deaf ear to what Ram had said. They kept following him at his heels. When they reached the bank of River Tamsa, darkness began to prevail. So, Sumant, the prime minister, stopped the chariot and decided to stay there for the night. All the people fell fast asleep soon due to fatigue and sorrow. When it was midnight, Ram said to Sumant, "Get the chariot ready. We must leave this place before these people get up otherwise they will never leave us."

Sumant did as Ram had said and the chariot moved on with Ram, Lakshman and Sita in it.

2

Travelling southwards, they crossed the Tamsa, the Ved Shruti and the Gomati and reached the southern boundary of the Kosala kingdom. Turning his face towards Ayodhya, Ram folded his hands and bowed his head in reverence saying, "I take leave of you, O Motherland. At the expiry of the period of exile, I shall again see you and my dear parents."

Proceeding further, the chariot reached the northern bank of the Ganga. This region was under Nishadraj, the chief of the *Nishads*. He was a class-mate of Ram at Saint Vasishtha's hermitage. When he came to know of Ram's arrival, his joy knew no bounds. He collected his chiefs and said, "Have you heard that my friend as well as master – Ram – has come. Let us go and receive him with open arms. Even a glance cast at his face is sure to rid us of all our sins and difficulties.

Nishadraj went to receive Ram, Lakshman and Sita. Then folding his hands, he said, "Let me know, Master, what can I do for you ? Your visit has really made this place sacred and pious."

"Your love has won me over. Do a favour to me as well. Arrange for a boat so that we may cross the Ganga and get to its southern bank." Saying so, Ram embraced Nishadraj.

When the chief of the Nishads went away to arrange for a boat, Ram said to Sumant, "Sir, you must return to Ayodhya now as we shall begin our exile from here."

"I can't dare to return to Ayodhya with my chariot empty. I have decided to stay in the forest and serve you day and night," retorted Sumant.

"No, sir. You must go back and do two important jobs – to console my father and to assure Mother Kaikayee that I have really started a forest life."

When Sumant had proceeded back to Ayodhya, Ram came to the ferry but the boatman refused to carry him across the river. Folding his hands, he said, "My Lord! I have heard that the touch of your feet has a magical effect. Anything touching them turns into a woman. Is it true that a rock turned into a woman on touching your feet? My boat is made of wood only. If it changes into a woman, my family is sure to starve."

Ram smiled and said, "How can your doubt be set at rest, friend ? Let me know."

"I won't let you step into my boat until and unless I wash your feet." retorted the boatman.

"All right ; wash my feet and get us across at once," said Ram.

The boatman washed Ram's feet with the water of the Ganga.

Having set his doubt at rest, the boatman made Ram, Lakshman and Sita sit in his boat and began to row it towards the other bank. Nishadraj was also in the boat at that time.

Reaching the other bank, all the four got down. The boatman lay prostrate at Ram's feet. Ram felt that he must pay the boatman his wages and so Sita took off her gold ring and handing it across to the boatman said, "Here is your wages."

"I have already got it." Saying so, the boatman folded his hands and said, "The wash of Lord Ram's feet is much more than my wages. It has done away with all my sins, sorrows and difficulties. So, I don't want anything now."

Bidding farewell to the boatman, Rama worshipped Lord Shiva while Sita implored the Ganga, "Mother Ganga ! bless me so that all my desires are fulfilled.

6

Ram, accompanied by his brother, wife and friend Nishadraj, crossed the dense forest and came to Prayag, a town at the confluence of Ganga and Yamuna. They visited the hermitage of Saint Bhardwaj who entertained them duly in every way. Then providing them seats to sit on, he said to Ram, "My meditation, seclusion and penance have attained completion today. My life has bloomed indeed to see you. No desire is left in my mind at all.

"He is really great and noble who is held in high esteem by you, O Saint !" Saying so, Ram implored, "Kindly suggest us some place where we can stay in peace."

The saint said, "There is a hillock named Chitrakoot across the Yamuna. That place is full of flower-plants, fruit trees, springs, waterfalls and other beauties of nature. In my opinion that place is most suitable for you to stay."

So, taking leave of Saint Bhardwaj, Ram proceeded to Chitrakoot.

Sumanta, on reaching Ayodhya, left the empty chariot outside the town. He dared not enter the town as if he had been guilty of murdering a Brahmana, a saint or a cow. He could not take courage to go into the capital during the day-time. So, he passed the day under a big tree and entered the town at night under the cover of darkness. Saving himself from the eyes of the people, he made for the royal palace and was directed to Queen Kaushalya's apartment by a maid. There King Dashratha was smarting under the sorrow of separation from his dear son. Bowing low, he greeted the king.

The king asked him, "How is my Ram, O Sumant ? Has he returned along with Sita and Lakshmana or not ? If not, make me reach there in the forest too. otherwise I shall certainly die."

Hearing this, Sumanta broke into tears and no words could come out of his throat.

Then seeing the king in untold sorrow, Sumant consoled him saying, "My Lord ! you are a store-house of true knowledge and also rank among top warriors. Your patience is immense indeed which you have developed as a result of your company with great saints and hermits. Joy and sorrow, company and separation, are subject to deeds and fate of a man. So, I'll request you to have fortitude and say good-bye to all sorrow and worry."

"You are right, dear. Everything is in the control of deeds and fate. My deed that earned the curse of the blind father of Shravana has borne fruit. Now I am fully convinced that I am fated to die of separation from my dear son."

The king was, in fact, reminded of the curse inflicted on him by Shravana's blind parents. Queen Kaushalya, on hearing about the curse, insisted on knowing the story about the curse and the king began to narrate it.

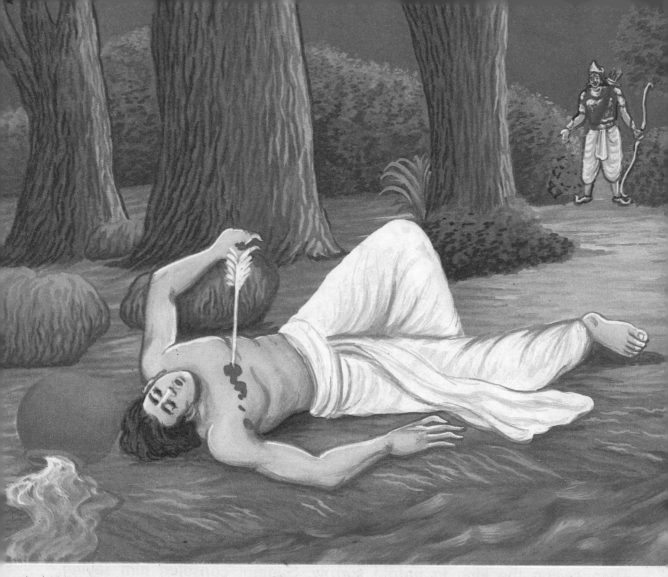

"One day I went out hunting into the Betas Forest. I sat on the branch of a tree that stood on the bank of a tank. It was a dark night. Shravana came to fill his jug with water from the tank. As soon as he put his jug into water, a gargling sound was produced. I took this sound for that of a deer. I am expert in shooting arrows on sound, you know. So, I shot an arrow on the gargling sound. It hit Shravana and he fell down on the ground with a loud cry – Oh God. The cry startled me and I ran to where it had come from. Seeing Shravana in a critical condition, I felt very hurt and repentant as well."

"Shravana said to me, It is no time to feel sorry. My old and blind parents are very thirsty. I had come in search of water for them. Carry this water to them so that they may quench their thirst. Tell them the whole story when they have drunk water. Saying so, Shravana breathed his last."

"Taking the jug of water I went where the old couple was. I told them the entire story and asked them to drink water. But they refused to take it and began to bewail in sorrow. Then they asked me to prepare a pyre which I did. The old couple sat on the pyre with their dead son in their laps. At the same time, they uttered a curse on me, "Listen O King! you will also die of separation from your son as we are doing now."

"At that time I had no son. So, I thought that the old couple had uttered a curse on me which will have no effect as I had no son then. But now when Ram, Lakshman and Sita are away to the forest, I have been reminded of the curse. I love Ram more than I love my life. He is away and I cannot survive without him. Death is staring me in my face indeed."

11

Having narrated the story of the curse to the queen, the king called out to Ram in a loud voice and then breathed his last.

All the three queens sat bewailing and the entire royal palace was plunged into sorrow. Even servants and maids sat mourning for the departed king. The news of the king's death spread like wild fire and the entire town of Ayodhya wore a sorrowful look. People began to say, "The king was a storehouse of righteousness, noble qualities and justice. He is no more now."

All the people began to curse Queen Kaikayee. Some of them abused her too. But the king had left this immortal world in sorrow for his son.

The night passed off and at day-break Saint Vasishtha was informed of the king's death.

Saint Vasishtha came running to the palace. He consoled the queens and the ministers with his religious sermons about death which is inevitable. Then he asked Sumant to put the king's body in a boat-like container filled with oil so that it should not decay.

Then Vasishtha sent for a messenger and asked him to go to Bharata who was with his mother's parents. He advised him not to disclose the news of the king's death there. He directed him to inform Bharata and Shatrughana that he (Vasishtha) had sent for them. He was sure that they would rush to Ayodhya when they get this message.

So, the messenger left for the town where Queen Kaikayee's parents lived so that he might bring back the two princes.

13

Now listen about Bharata. He had been seeing ominous happenings since the things had started deterioracting at Ayodhya. So, his mind was always suspicious of some calamity to befall. He often saw bad dreams and so he meditated hard praying to the Almighty for the safety and happiness of all kith and kin. Just then, Vasishtha's messenger reached there and conveyed the saint's message that he wanted them both to rush to Ayodhya at their earliest.

So, Bharat took leave of his maternal grand-parents and after worshipping his gods he proceeded to Ayodhya in a chariot along with Shatrughna. Their minds were at Ayodhya now. They wished to fly to their home-town indeed.

When the two princes reached near Ayodhya, things did not appear well to them. Ominous things like howling of jackals, braying of asses and weeping of dogs happened. On entering the town, they found it plunged in sorrow. The people who came across their way, looked dejected. Everyone simply greeted them and went away without uttering a word.

Seeing everything against his expectations Bharata got suspicious and drove straight to his royal apartment. Then he asked his wife Mandavi, "Is everything all right here ?"

"See your mother first of all," replied the prince-consort, "She must be eagerly waiting for you." Saying so, Mandavi left the place and Bharata made for his mother's palace.

Having known that Bharata had come, Kaikayee came to the door of his palace to receive him delightfully in the proper religious way. Then he took his son inside her palace and asked, "Is everything all right there?"

"Yes, everything is all right there. But what about here? How is dear father and the other two queen-mothers. Are my elder brother and his wife Sita all right? Where is Lakshmana, my brother?" Bharata put a volley of questions to Kaikayee so that he might know the reality.

Hearing his son's queries, Kaikayee filled her eyes with crocodile tears and said, "You know, it was I who safe-guarded your interests well in time. Manthra too helped me a lot in this task. But one sad thing happened that your father died suddenly.

Hearing about the death of his father, Bharata began to bewail bitterly. He asked his mother to explain how the death had occurred.

Kaikayee told all the story to his son – how she had manipulated to get the throne for him and exile for Ram with Manthra's help. Then she added, "My son ! it does not become a king to shed tears. Be up and enjoy the comforts that God has showered on you."

Bharata got enraged to hear the words of his mother and said,"You sinful lady ! you have done irreparable harm to our family. Why didn't you strangle me to death when I was born. I am ashamed of having you as my mother. A father like King Dashratha and brothers like Ram and Lakshmana – where shall I get them ? I disown you as my mother."

Just then, Manthra came there in her best clothes and ornaments. Shatrughna got enraged to see her and kicked him so hard at her back that she fell down on the ground. Her hunch broke and her head was also broken. She exclaimed in pain, "O God ! Is this the repayment of my good done to Bharata ?"

17

Leaving Kaikayee's palace, both the princes went to Queen Kaushalya's palace. Seeing the king's corpse there, they began to bewail bitterly.

Seeing the princes weeping bitterly, Saint Vasishtha said to Bharata, "Dear Bharat! birth and death; joy and sorrow– all are natural laws. A person who takes birth on this earth, must die one day. So, give up your sorrow and prepare for the funeral rites of the late king."

"Yes sir," said Bharata. He got up with a heavy heart and ordered Sumanta to make preparations for the last rites of the king.

The pyre was ready in no time and the last obsequies of King Dashratha were performed in keeping with the directions given in religious scriptures.

18

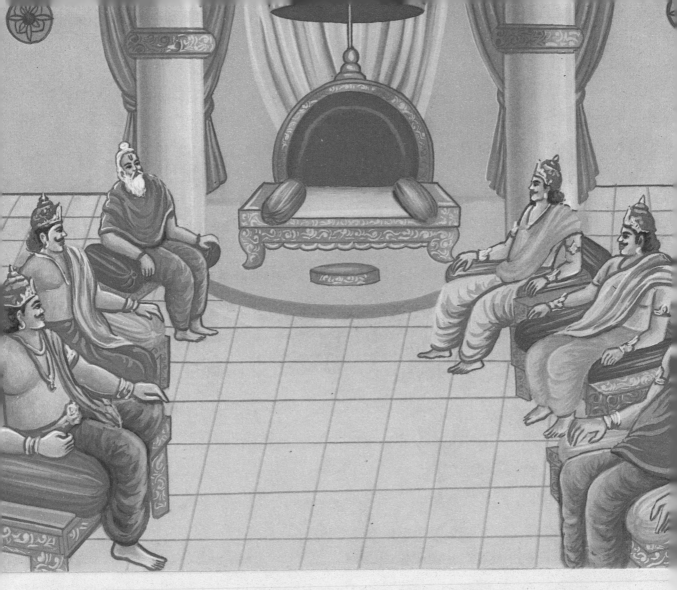

Now Bharata held his court where all the nobles and ministers were present along with Saint Vasishtha. Giving a sermon on the balance between religion and politics, Vasishtha said, "Bharat ! what is to be, must be. Birth and death, gain and loss, fame and defame – are all in God's hands. King Dashrath led a life full of luck and all comforts. Shed all sorrow and obey your father's wishes. Accept the throne and serve your subjects."

All the nobles and ministers too supported what Saint Vasishtha had said. Hearing these words Bharata said in a humble voice, "O Great Saint ! you are our family preceptor. It is said that a king must be religious and honest. But as for me, I am a grave sinner. My father died because of me. My two brothers and sister-in-law had to go into exile only due to me. How can I accept this throne. It is Ram's... and only he will mount it. This is my pledge."

Taking the pledge to enthrone Ram, Bharata implored all present in the court, "If you all have good wishes for the kingdom, you must help me fulfil my pledge. Let us all go to the forest and coronate Ram there itself and then we can prevail upon him to return to Ayodhya. I am sure, he will not kick me. He must accept my request."

Everyone supported Bharata's suggestion and so Sumanta made arrangements for the march to the forest just as Bharata had ordered.

Next day, Bharata left for the forest accompanied by his kith and kin, nobles, ministers, and Saint Vasishtha. Articles to be used for the coronation were also carried along.

King Janaka, Sita's father, too joined Bharata in this great march along with his kith and kin and soldiers.

Ram, Lakshmana and Sita had started living in a hut at Chitrakoot.

One day, all the three were sitting before the hut when they saw birds flying about hither and thither in fright. Ram said to Lakshmana, "Birds are flying about in fright. Not only this, clouds of dust can also be seen rising in the horizon. Just watch what the matter is."

Hearing this, Lakshmana climbed up a tall tree and watched carefully. Then he spoke in a voice full of suspicion, "Be ready, brother ! After capturing the throne, Bharat is coming here with his army with a view to getting rid of us."

"No, never, Lakshmana. Your doubt is unfounded. Bharat is very righteous. He cannot do like that Let him reach here and you will come to know of the reality," said Rama serenely.

Having reached Chitrakoot, when Bharata came to know of Rama's hut, he ran to embrace his brother. Seeing Bharata running bare-footed, Ram too ran towards him and said, "Dear brother! You... here! Is everything all right?"

"Dear brother!" Saying so Bharata embraced Rama. Seeing this, Lakshmana felt sorry for his suspicion. He said to himself, "How wrongly I assess things sometimes! Bharat loves Ram as dearly as I do."

So, Lakshmana begged for Bharata's pardon who embraced him too. Then paying his respects to Sita, Bharata expressed the purpose of his visit.

Just then came there all the three widowed queens. Seeing them in widows' dresses, Rama began to bewail bitterly.

Bharata said to Rama, "Dear Father could not bear the sorrow of separation from you, brother. He breathed his last with your name on his lips. I was with my maternal parents at that time."

"Oh Dear Father !" exclaimed Rama in sorrow and then said, "I hoped to return to Ayodhya at the expiry of the period of exile. But with dear father's departure, my enthusiasm has disappeared."

Then Saint Vasishtha advised Ram a lot and consoled him as well. So, Ram stood in waters of the Mandakini and offered oblations to the departed soul of his father saying, "This pious water should ever keep reaching you."

Next day, Bharata placed before Ram the royal robe and other articles of

coronation and said, "We have come to crown you king here."

"I can never do so, dear brother," retorted Ram.

"But why after all ?" asked Bharata.

"Because I am bound by the boons given by dear father to Mother Kaikayee," replied Ram.

"If a person must live in exile for fourteen years to keep the boon of dear father, I am here to do it," suggested Bharata.

"No, dear, Bharat. According to his boons, I am to live in exile while you are to mount the throne. So you must run the government till I am in exile," argued Ram.

"All right; if this is your wish, I must run the administration but in your name only. These wooden shoes of yours will be placed on the throne as a token." Saying so, Bharata returned to Ayodhya with Ram's wooden shoes.

Printed at :
Seema Printing Works